I0221392

Ronald Sutherland Gower

**Notes of a Tour from Brindisi to Yokohama**

1883-1884

Ronald Sutherland Gower

**Notes of a Tour from Brindisi to Yokohama**
*1883-1884*

ISBN/EAN: 9783744662659

Printed in Europe, USA, Canada, Australia, Japan

Cover: Foto ©Andreas Hilbeck / pixelio.de

More available books at **www.hansebooks.com**

# NOTES OF A TOUR FROM

# BRINDISI TO YOKOHAMA

## 1883—1884

BY

## LORD ·RONALD GOWER

"Voyager, c'est apprendre."—ANON.

LONDON
KEGAN PAUL, TRENCH & CO.
MDCCCLXXXV

THESE NOTES ARE DEDICATED

TO MY FRIEND

GOWER ROBINSON,

IN RECOLLECTION OF PLEASANT DAYS PASSED

TOGETHER IN JAPAN.

R. G.

# *N O T E.*

I HAVE requested my obliging publishers to make this little book of pocket size, so that it may perhaps be of use to travellers making a similar tour.

# CONTENTS.

# NOTES OF A TOUR

## BRINDISI TO YOKOHAMA,

### 1883–84.

### CHAPTER I.

#### FROM BRINDISI TO BOMBAY.

*On board s.s. "Mongolia"* (*P. & O. Co.*),
*Nov.* 13. — We (an old Cambridge friend,
E. ff. Mathews, and myself) have had since
leaving Brindisi yesterday a gloriously fine
and calm voyage. We are now running by
the island of Crete. Last Sunday we looked
about that most intensely uninteresting town
of Brindisi. On Monday we had a splendid
day for seeing the rocky isles of Cephalonia
and Zante, which lay some miles to the east,
bathed in sunny mist. A few Anglo-Indians
among the passengers, also a sprinkling of

**A**

Turks and Germans; few of the military element.

Port Said was reached on the morning of the 15th. There we remained till the evening, when we steamed on to Alexandria. We have decided to give up the Suez Canal journey, and go by the overland route to Suez; this will give us more time in Cairo.

*Port Said, Nov.* 15.—I am glad to set foot first in classic Alexandria, and not in this wretchedly uninteresting place; an ugly harbour, with a lighthouse and some out-buildings to keep it company.

That evening the sunset was of marvellous beauty, the western sky of a deep glowing orange hue, covered with fleecy saffron-coloured clouds. As these glories paled, the moon rose. Coming on deck before sunrise next day, I found the sky of a deep purple colour; gradually the purple faded, and now, before what seemed a rivalry between the growing dawn and the still brilliant moon, the sunrise was even more glorious than had been the sunset. I certainly never remember seeing as one did that day the shadows cast by the two rival lights of night and day.

We landed early at Alexandria, when we found three hours ample for seeing the place. An Egyptian, in a dark-blue uniform relieved with silver lace, escorted us. Even Paris immediately after the Commune had no scene of more wanton and thorough destruction to show than the principal Square of Alexandria. The pulverised forts are eloquent of the progress of Western over Eastern civilisation. Leaving Alexandria at three, we reached Cairo at nine that evening. *Czech's (late Shepherd) Hotel.*—Here it is as hot as on an average day in July in England. This comfortable hotel is lively with English officers; some wearing the Egyptian fez, young E. Stuart Wortley, for instance. He is A.D.C. to Sir E. Baring, and has seen hard work here, not only in the field, but where true courage is more necessary, namely, in the hospitals full of cholera cases. He tells me that he and his chief literally walked the hospitals while the cholera was at its worst three times daily. The native doctors were worse than useless.[1] We visited the Turkish bazaar, dirty and picturesque, but less so than Algiers. We have also visited Boulak on donkey-back—a disgust-

[1] S. W. told me, *à propos* of these doctors, that they would get as far away as possible from their patients, and examine them through opera-glasses!

ingly dirty suburb of Cairo, but containing
in its museum the rarest collection of Egyptian antiquities in the world. Founded
by Mariette, it contains an astounding collection of relics of the Pharaohs—kings
and queens by the score, and even the
mummy of the great Sesostris himself! My
first view of the Pyramids—unforgettable
sight—was from the fashionable drive, the
Shoubra, which is to Cairo what the Champs
Elysées are to Paris and Hyde Park to
London. Here all Cairo comes out in the
afternoon, in carriage, on horseback, or afoot.
Although the scene is gay, it has lost most
of its chief attractions since the reign of
Ismail the Magnificent. The Khedive
drove by in an open carriage, attended by
a rather seedy-looking escort. He has a soft,
effeminate, Frenchified type of face, and does
not look the man to guide this country in so
difficult a crisis. He is said to be fairly intelligent. The only Egyptian of high official
position that I came into contact with was
Scherif Pâcha, a most agreeable, talkative old
" Boulvadier " type of man. He told me of
his fears respecting General Hicks' expedition
(soon to be so sadly realised). Of the English
then in Cairo, I saw most of Edgar Vincent,

newly arrived to try and set the financial
difficulties of the country into some order,
in which hard task he has been successful.
He occupied a room in the hotel, which he had
brightened by gorgeous stuffs and hangings
brought from Constantinople, among which
he looked like a young prince out of the
Arabian Nights.

We passed pleasant evenings at the pretty
little villa of the Fitzgeralds ; he a distinguished Indian officer, and his wife a daugh-
ter of Lord Houghton, a friend of several
years' standing.  We visited and climbed to
the top of the Great Pyramid, and tried in vain
to discover any expression on the battered
face of the Sphinx, and exhausted most of
the sights of the place.  One ascension we
made was an uncommon one ; this was in a
balloon belonging to an aeronaut of the
name of Simmons.  Mr. Simmons was rash
enough to make a non-captive ascent (ours
had been a captive ascent) ; descended late at
night many miles out in the desert, and on
returning to fetch his balloon next day, found
not a trace of it.  No one wishing to have
the best view of Cairo should fail to ascend
to the citadel about sundown, and watch the
effect from the Mameluke terrace, as the

afterglow spreads over what I think Thackeray called "one of the noblest views on earth." When you have seen that, you may as well leave Cairo, for there is nothing to compare to it.

Being rather hurried to go on our way to India, we had no time for making further expeditions. In order to see anything of the Nile, at least a month is required. We had seen sufficient to make one wish to pass an entire winter in this wonderful land, the most interesting, historically, that exists. After a couple of weeks at Cairo, we pursued our journey, going by train to Suez. Owing to a delay, it was quite dark when we passed Tel-el-Kebir. One could only dimly discern a very few tombstones placed in a dreary enclosure, looking like one of those forlorn graveyards which are so common in Scotland.

*On board P. & O. s.s. "Brindisi."* — At noon we left Suez in a steam-launch, under a blazing sun for two hours before we boarded this vessel. A large warship, crowded with troops, passed this morning on her way to Tonquin, presaging war and trouble to the French for many a day to come. The long ranges of the

Arabian hills, as the sun set, glowed with a deep rosy colour, and a deeper crimson reigned when the sun had disappeared—the afterglow which has struck all travellers in the East, and which appears this 'winter to be more brilliant than ordinary. Slowly faded away the land of the Pharaohs; the stars came out from the purple vault with a brilliancy that is not to be realised unless one has seen these southern latitudes; darkness succeeded the rich glow of the sunset, and Mount Sinai was invisible in the gathered gloom as we steamed down into the Red Sea. Aden was reached at dawn on the 6th (December). I was reminded of Hong-Kong in the volcanic shape of its arid hills; the utter want of any verdure gives an almost ghastly look to the place. Some nuns came on board; they belong to the order of the "Good Shepherd." We visited their establishment at the end of the crescent-shaped row of buildings which is the principal feature of this town, if town Aden can be called. There are five sisters in all; the Superior reminded me, in manner and appearance, of our Queen. They were most courteous, and we could not but admire their charity and devotion in toiling in so arid a spot as Aden.   One of the sisters has been here eight years.

The natives are a fine-looking race, well-featured, and men of muscle, of a deep-chocolate hue; some with shorn heads: some of the boys, bright, intelligent lads, with sparkling eyes and fine teeth; these, like at Honolulu, came out to the ship's sides in their little canoes, and loudly shouted for coins to be thrown in the sea, after which they plunged, and never failed to catch them as they sank into the water.

Between Aden and Bombay is a blank; the most intrepid journalists can have nothing more interesting to note than the ship's run, the books they have read, the acquaintances, perhaps friendships, they have made on board.

# CHAPTER II.

EARLY on the 12th (January) we arrived in the harbour of Bombay, and set foot on India's "coral strand." Many hours were uncomfortably passed in the custom-house, where no kind of order is maintained. We had an invitation to stay at the Byculla Club, but on finding the distance that it is from the landing-place, we elected to put up at a huge caravansary called Watson's, or the Esplanade Hotel—a large building, half shops, half hotel, and altogether detestable.

We passed four days in Bombay, and most interesting days these were.

From the Governor, Sir James Fergusson, we met with great civility; and had our stay been longer, we would have accepted his kind invitation to be his guests.

Our first expedition was to the famed caves

of Elephanta. These are reached in a steam tug, about an hour's trip from Bombay, across one of the finest harbours in the world. The sculptures without and within the caves are most curious here as elsewhere in India. The resemblance of these sculptured temples to that of a far older race than the Hindoos, namely, the Mexicans, is very apparent. Elephanta is the great picnic resort of the people of Bombay, an Indian Burnham Beeches; and scenes where gods were worshipped, and human sacrifices performed in former times, are now consecrated to the eating of sandwiches and lobsters, and the worship of Bass and of Mumm. The native town of Bombay is full of picturesque features, but the buildings are generally "baroque" in style. The whole scene is like some gigantic fair. The Government buildings impose by their size, but are not architectural triumphs. Gothic may be suited to the shores of the Thames, but is out of keeping in the East. What interested me most here has been seeing cremation as practised by the natives; also that weird form of burial, or devoural, as practised by the Parsees, in the Towers of Silence. The former mode of returning a body to its dust is, I think, by far the most

sensible—infinitely better than our perni-
cious mode of burying our friends in leaden
coffins, which necessarily prevents, perhaps
for centuries, the purifying earth to come
together with the decaying body. Our mode
of burial has already caused in thousands of
cases pestilence in the midst of our towns
and villages. Remember the life of Charlotte
Brontë for one instance. One would have
thought that the very horror of putrefaction
would cause rational beings to transform into
harmless ashes the bodies of the dead; but
the Church has ordained that bodies should
not be burnt, and we consequently keep near
our dwellings the decaying corpses of millions,
poisoning our springs, and now and again
giving unmistakable proofs of the folly of
making the living suffer, merely because
some eighteen hundred years ago it was
found necessary to stow away under ground
the corpses of the early followers of Christ.

A courteous Hindoo, Mr. Raghoonath
Narrayen, did us the honours of the Hindoo
cremation grounds. The cremations take
place within a high-walled open space, half
garden, half yard, close by the carriage-road
near the sea, a road named Rotten, probably
from its being used by equestrians. Some

ten corpses were under process of burning; there was but little smell, and that little not offensive; and although it may sound rather horrible to see so many bodies all more or less reduced to ashes, there was curiously little of the repugnant in the sight. Here the mourners, after bearing the body within the place of burning, leave it to be reduced to ashes; some generally, we were told, remain as a mark of respect. To see our dearest friend thus burnt must be a painful duty; but about death and what follows as regards the poor human shell, there must be always much that is unavoidably painful to the survivors. However, cremation, as carried out here in the rudest and simplest form, made me more strongly in favour of it than ever; and although I have but little hope of seeing such a mode of burial practised in our country, I still look forward to the day when some high dignitary, a Bishop for instance, would at least after his death make himself of some use, and have cremation practised on his body, and by his shining example give countenance to the most civilised and sensible way of returning dust to dust, ashes to ashes!

The Parsee mode of burial is outwardly more impressive; the very name "Towers of

Silence" has something grand and eloquent about it; and these great Mamelons, placed in the midst of a park-like eminence overlooking the city and the sea, have a lofty air about them, very different to the lowly yard where the Hindoo dead are disposed of. Here, too, there is a solemnity and almost melodramatic effect admirably suited to the dignified and singularly cultured race who carry out their funeral rights with much pomp and circumstance. The mourners, clothed in long white flowing robes, pass majestically along, and after leaving the body within one of the towers,—for there are several scattered about the gardens,—slowly return, accompanied by a little dog, who has been made to gaze into the eyes of the corpse, thereby, according to Parsee belief, extracting the sins of the departed. Round the top of the circular towers immense vultures are seated in grisly rows, waiting their daily repast.

No one having time to spare should fail to go to Poonah from Bombay—an expedition of six hours by rail. The scenery traversed is most beautiful—the famed Ghauts, with fertile valleys at their feet. The Poonah Club, where we remained a couple of days, is a most luxurious one. There we were received by Colonel Burnett, one of the most courteous and agreeable of colonels. The two days passed at Poonah were ample for us to see the chief sight, viz., the Mosque or Temple of Parvati, overlooking the plain and battlefield of Kirkee. Priests were praying in miniature chapels, and chanting their hymns, and around the summit of the towers bright-green parrots chirped and twittered as they clung gracefully on the ruined walls of the old Peshwa's palace. Government House is worthy of a visit, for its gardens are beautiful; full of splendid roses and large convolvuli. The bazaars are full of large-turbaned natives. The native town is divided into seven parts, each named after a day in the week. The old palace of the Janawadu was the scene of the public executions down to the reign of Baji Rao; criminals were trampled to death by elephants. There is an admirably-arranged jail, containing nearly a thousand prisoners, many of which make handsome carpets. The caves of Karli are well worth seeing. Two hours' rail brings one to the station (Lanoli). Hence it is a half-hour's drive to the place where the road ends, and a path leads across a flat plain to the rocks containing these caverns. It was a very hot two miles' walk, and at the end we had a steep ascent; but the really extraordinary appearance of the caves amply repaid us the trouble. Though not to compare in beauty of situation to those of Elephanta, the Karli caves are more intricate in laborious design and vaster in depth and height. I believe that these rock-cut temples, of whose history so little is known, are the finest in India next to those of Elura. While we were visiting the caves an encampment of the 4th Foot had established itself near the bungalow where we had left our carriage. We found the officers a pleasant set of young men. Colonel Stokes took us over the camp. A bit of local colour was a park of a dozen elephants, who seemed to be enjoying their rest after their march.

Next day we returned to Bombay. Dinners with the Governor at his distant house at Parell, and with the most genial of officials, Sir Frank Souter,[1] whose acquaintance no

---

[1] I had the pleasure of meeting at Sir Frank's one evening at dinner one of the most intelligent of that highly-cultured race the Parsis, Mr. Dosabhai Framgi, whose book on his fellow-countrymen and the tenets of Zoroaster is well worth reading. I am glad to see that a new and enlarged edition of this work has recently (1884) been published by Messrs. Macmillan & Co.

one should fail to make when visiting
Bombay, and who seems as popular among
the natives as with Europeans, followed.   On
the evening of the 23rd we took the train,
reaching Ahmedabad early next day.   The
speed of travelling by rail in India will be
judged when it takes fourteen hours to go 310
miles.   At Ahmedabad we were received and
sheltered in a large bungalow by a friend (T.
Mackonochie), who, although but fresh from
Oxford, has in this district, in his quality of
civil servant to H.B.M., more power than any
lord-lieutenant of an English county.

Ahmedabad is the most interesting native
town we had yet seen.   Here were no Europeans to take off from the purely Indian appearance of the dark human tide which crowded the
streets of this city, the second in importance
to that of Bombay in that province.   During
a stay of three days at Ahmedabad we received
much hospitality from Mr. (Justice) Crawford
and his wife ; we also messed with Colonel
Hadow at the Artillery depôt.   At first it seems
strange to tiffin and dine daily with those
whom we have never known before ; but in
India one is welcomed by strangers as old
friends, and if it were only to see the best
side of the English character in the way of

hospitality, a visit to India would amply repay one. I believe, as a rule, travellers give Ahmedabad the go-by as they hurry north; but for any one interested in the art and architecture of Hindustan a couple of days should certainly be passed there. The town itself is full of fine architectural remains; grand old towers and walls surround it; and the wondrously carved stone windows of Sidi Seyzid's Mosque are among the very finest, if not the very most remarkable specimen of stone-carving in India. The red sandstone has been so deftly carved and cut, that it appears in these windows like the finest lace work, and the design of waving palm trees is as graceful as the work is delicate and minute. Besides this mosque there are many others of beauty and interest within the town walls; that of Shalis Bagh, for instance, built about 1700 by a Guzerat king; the superb and recently restored one of Muhufiz Khan; the Jumna Musjid, with its forest of columns; the one of Rani Lipris, small but beautiful; and the grandest of all, that of Shah Alam, with its vast terraced front, superbly carved tombs, shaded by an immense single palm-tree that adds grace to the whole scene. Here, too, are an interesting series of tombs of the family of Ahmed Shah, and of

B

that monarch in elaborately carved alabaster.
These things within the town take a day to
visit; but in the neighbourhood of Ahmedabad are still more splendid memorials of the
former rulers of this portion of India.   There
is a well, or rather a succession of underground
wells, within the most beautiful walls that one
can imagine; there are seven in all, each more
elaborately sculptured than the former.   But
the wonder of wonders near Ahmedabad is
certainly the old pleasure palace of the kings,
named Sarchez, built in the fifteenth century
by Mahmud Bagaru.   This glorious old pile
lies some six miles west of the city.   Looking
back on my visit to India, and after seeing
the far more famous structures at Delhi and
Agra, I return to my conviction when I stood
on the colossal flight of steps which lead into
a large lake before the palace, flanked by
an apparently endless row of temples and
palaces; that nothing in point of splendour,
and in the realisation of all one has dreamt
of the former magnificence of the Eastern
monarchs, can more realise those dreams
than this place.   It is like one of Martin's
or Danby's pictures realised; with a back-
ground that would have suited the visit
of the Queen of Sheba to Solomon, or the

revels of Sardanapalus. We had started
before daylight in order to pass as much of
the day as we could spare in exploring this
wondrous old palace, and in wandering
amidst the marble-floored halls and temples
where rest those that once made these de-
solate old halls a dream of splendour. Now
they are given over to dolorous creatures, and
echo only the ghostly laugh of the hyena as
the night closes around.

On the following day we went to Baroda,
Mackonochie coming with us and introducing
us to Major Howard Mellis—a perfect host
and a most genial, who acts the part of Lieu-
tenant-General in that pleasant city. We
found a smart carriage of the Gaikwar's
waiting, with native coachman and footman
in immense red turbans. "We are here
most comfortably installed in a beautiful
bungalow belonging to Mr. Elliot, former
Governor to the Gaikwar. Baroda is the most
home-like looking place we have seen yet in
India ; its rows of beautifully kept gardens,
with the neat villa-like buildings, and the
park-like grounds around the Residency,
where General Watson lives, give an almost
English happy village-like look to the place."

As we had the honour of being presented

to the Gaikwar, who struck us as being a
most promising young prince, it may be well
to add a few lines about him.   Born in 1863,
his short history is somewhat romantic.   His
name in full is Maharajah Sivaji Rao; he is
the direct descendant, although he passed
his childhood in poverty, through a younger
son of Pilaji Rao, the founder of the family
of Rao.   On the deposition of the late
Gaikwar (Mulhar Rao), in 1874, for being
supposed to have attempted to poison
Colonel Phayre, the present Gaikwar was
adopted by a princess of the house as her
son, and he has now succeeded to his ancestors' dominions.   That his education has
been carefully undertaken is evident, and
the general impression is that Mr. Elliot has
had great success in his charge.   Formerly
Baroda was famous for the sports and shows
given on certain occasions by the Gaikwar, in
which animals more or less wild were pitted
against one another, "mais on a changé tout
cela," and instead of seeing tigers and
elephants attacking each other we were
treated by the Gaikwar to an entertainment
in which a German conjurer performed some
familiar tricks.   We regretted not seeing the
"wild sports of the arena," but were bound

to admire the Gaikwar's humanity and the softening influence of European teaching. Nothing can be imagined more hideous than the style of furnishing that one invariably sees in the palaces of native princes in India ;[1] and it is to be hoped that in an immense palace now building for the Gaikwar, and which is to cost some quarter of a million, more taste will be shown. Of diamonds the young prince has a priceless collection ; in a row of brilliants, the central one is the " Star of the South." He has also " ropes of pearls," such as Lord Beaconsfield was so fond of writing about in his novels, but until I had seen those at Baroda I had not believed in.

Our visit to the Gaikwar was of interest. We drove some six miles to a hideously ugly, liver-coloured, barrack-like building, where, until the new palace is finished, the Prince resides during the summer. We were shown into a small building on one side of the court-yard facing the palace. In a few moments the Gaikwar, with a large red umbrella borne over him, and, with the exception of his head-dress, in European costume, rapidly crossed the yard and entered the room where we were wait-

---

[1] Almost needless to say that what is ugly in India is of English manufacture.

ing. He gives one the impression of being intelligent and amiable, and his expression is a good one. In every way he seems a great contrast to his predecessor. We were entertained by a Mohammedan magnate at his house, at the entrance of which six mounted soldiers were drawn up, and we were received with much ceremony. A nautch dance was gone through, and anything more ungraceful or hideous than the posturing and shrieking of the three performers, two young and an old woman, would be difficult to imagine. Before leaving, our hands were smeared with some evil-smelling, sticky compound and garlands placed round our shoulders.

The state elephants we also inspected, and had the honour of a ride on a gigantic brute whose body was adorned with crimson and golden stuffs, and a golden howdah on its back.

Returning for a night to Ahmedabad, we left the following evening for Jeypore, where we arrived early next day, on the first of the new year (1884). We called on Dr. Stratton, the Resident, who lives in a pleasant villa, in the midst of an Italian-looking garden, with cypresses, &c. ; and have seen the Maharajah's huge palace, with its immense hall, in which he holds his durbars; the stables, with four hundred horses; also a very creditable school of arts, in which native talent is well displayed. Jeypore, or, as it is often spelt, Jaipoor ("City of Victory"), is most picturesque, with its wide straight streets, its rhubarb-coloured houses and walls, and its great palace towering over all; it is full of curiosities, and the elephants abound in its walls.

The great lion here is the Palace of Ambar, which, methinks, the French author Rousselet has not over-praised in his glowing description. Ambar is a day's ride from Jeypore. You drive away early from the comfortable Kaiser-i-hind Hotel for some half-a-dozen miles, through a valley literally covered with the ruins of ancient temples. Arriving at the foot of the cliff on which the castle rises, terrace over terrace, you leave the carriage and mount an elephant. After passing under many battlemented gateways, the outer-court is reached. For several hours we wandered through a maze of courts and along endless corridors. It is hardly an exaggeration to say of this place, that "beside it the wonders of Seville and Granada would appear insignificant." I was reminded at Ambar of

Heidelberg and of Ehrenbreitstein. From
the many coigns of vantage, one has glorious
prospects of the walled hills that rise at the
back of the castle, and of the vast plain
stretching for many miles, and the distant
hills that lie between us and Delhi. The
situation is grand beyond words, and days
might be passed here in merely going from
one exquisite room into another of this fairy-
like palace. Marble windows, an inch thick,
are carved through with the lightest and
most graceful designs; ceilings ablaze with
glass and gold, and huge doors of copper
glowing like burnished brass. An army
might be lodged within these courts, and
all Solomon's wives be stowed into these
inner gardens, fragrant with the perfume of
the orange and jasmine.

On the following day, after visiting the
armoury in the Palace at Jeypore (a fine
collection, but badly placed in little dark
rooms), we had another elephant ride to
the entrance of the Ghaut. A narrow road,
or rather a lane, lined on either side with
graceful galleries, minaret-crowned, leads
to the end of the valley from which the
wide plains, or rather desert, opens out. In
the far distance bold-shaped hills rise out of

a sea of desolation, looking like far-away islands in a yellow sea. The gardens will also repay a visit which border one side of the narrow path. Jeypore is indeed well worthy a few days being passed in it ; and it has one of the very few really comfortable inns in India.

Eleven hours' rail over a flat and unlovely plain brings the traveller to Delhi. The "Travellers' Bungalow" is not an uncomfortable one as bungalows go. The best general view of the Historic Ridge is to be had from the roof of Ludlow Castle, where Mr. Tremlett, the Resident, lives. He pointed out the principal features of the places made memorable during the siege. The old palace of the Delhi kings has been converted into hideous barracks, but the audience chamber, wherein stood the peacock throne and the private apartments, the walls of which are of white marble, with the most graceful of flower-like patterns, introduced in coloured marbles like the best *pietra dura* work, are superb. Unlike the Castle Palace of Ambar, there is no fine view from the Palace of Delhi, and the eye sweeps from out these marble-traceried windows over an arid yellow plain through which the sluggish Jumna flows. The gem of the palace buildings is the Pearl Mosque, a dream in white marble. There is a richness and also a simplicity in this little building that nothing can describe. Towering over the surrounding buildings is the immense Mosque of Jumna-Musjid, the most striking feature of Delhi. A month might profitably be passed at Delhi in examining the remains of the former splendour of the Great Mughuls, who here, from the beginning of the sixteenth century till an end was put to their rule in the Mutiny, built temple on temple, mosque upon mosque, palace on palace. A circumference of twenty miles encircles the ruins of this Indian Rome. Imagine all these buildings as they must have appeared when Aurangzeb the Splendid held here his state! Within the town the finest street is the Chandui Chouk (Silver Street), full of jewellers' shops of the most tempting description. Of all the mosques we had as yet seen none was to compare to the Jumna-Musjid, undoubtedly one of the finest and noblest buildings of the East. The rich warm colour of the sandstone of which the lower portion of this mosque is built contrasts admirably with the pure white marble of the bulbous-shaped domes with their gilded pinnacles flashing in the sun. Ascending the minaret on the left of the temple Delhi lies at your feet like a huge map. As a town Delhi is not nearly so picturesque as Jeypore. Every one at all interested in the Mutiny will visit the Historic Ridge and the Flagstaff Tower. One feels when travelling in India the want of a good guide to these historic scenes : the one published by Murray and written by East-wick is most unsatisfactory ; one is not told what is worth seeing, but only confused by a wearisome and endless list of places, of which the spelling alone is enough to bewilder the reader. As a rule it cannot matter much how Mr. Eastwick chooses to spell the names of Indian places ; but when he changes the well-known and universal way of spelling such historic places as Lucknow into "Lakknau," Delhi into "Dihli," and Cawn-pore into "Kánhpúr," his guide becomes a puzzle and a nuisance.

A long day—in fact many—can be profit-ably passed in visiting the superb Tomb of Humayan (Akbar's father) ; it is the West-minster Abbey of the Mughul royal house, built, like the Jumna-Musjid, of red sand-stone with marble domes. Its terraces and

neglected gardens cover a prodigious extent
of ground. It was from here that Hodson
took prisoners the sons of the King of Oude.
The drive from here to the wondrous red-
tower, the far-famed Kootab Minar, extends
for six miles through a country literally studded
with the tombs of kings and the remains of
ancient castles and towns. Before reaching
the Kootab visit the marble tombs and
mausoleums Mizamud diu Auliza—the well
into which men and boys fling themselves
from a height of forty feet; also the Tomb
of Safdar Jang—an imitation of the Taj at
Agra. You will of course be expected to
mount the Kootab Tower; the view from its
top amply repays one for the climb: it is 238
feet high, and rises, in five stories, from a
diameter of 47 to 9 feet. Authorities are in
doubt as to when it was built; it is probably
one of the most ancient, and certainly the
most important single structure in Hindustan. Beneath it are the remains of a
mosque, of half-Moorish, half-Hindoo architecture; and rising in the centre of a
ruined court is the mysterious iron pillar or
shaft of Raja Dhava, which is supposed to
belong to the third or fourth century A.D.
It is said to be as deep below ground as it is

above.   Altogether this day's sight-seeing is
one that leaves an impression on eye and
mind that is not easily forgotten.

A Turkish or rather Indian bath taken at
Delhi is also a thing not easily forgotten.  I
thought the way one was treated in a bath
at Cairo severe enough, but it was nothing
compared to the way in which at Delhi one
was twisted and turned, now with one's feet
over and behind one's head, and now with
the operator dancing a war-dance on one's
chest or back.   The monkeys that abound
in the park-like grounds near the Travellers'
Bungalow here are as tame as dogs with the
natives ; but as soon as they see a European
they decamp, and no wonder, as it seems
Tommy Atkins' habit to throw stones as they
pass at the inoffensive animals.   Agra is seven
hours' rail from Delhi.   We were comfortably
lodged at the Agra Club, a large and very
luxurious building.   Naturally the first place
we visited was the world-famed Taj-Mahal.
The Taj fully realised all that I had expected of it.   In its way it is absolute perfection ; perhaps, to be rather hypercritical, it
is too complete, too finished, too perfect.
The gardens above which it raises its domes
and minarets remind one of those in the

Generaliffe at Granada, and a little of some
of those in Oxford ; these add immensely to
the effect of the matchless tomb, which rises
in its pure white like a petrified fountain from
out an emerald lake. The interior as compared to the exterior seems a little dull and
plain ; the minarets, too, might appear somewhat like glorified lighthouses in form,
especially at their base ; but in spite of these
small drawbacks, the Taj is certainly one of
the most marvellous creations of human eye
and hand, and is worth alone the journey to
India to see; and it will hand down the
name of Shah Jahan to all the ages. Below
the terraces elephants were refreshing themselves in the Jumna, and natives in their
bright-coloured dresses gave picturesqueness
and colour to the scene. Not so, however, the
European tourists, who seemed out of place
in so purely Oriental a scene. We were fortunate in the time of our visit to Agra, for
to see the Taj aright it should be visited by
moonlight. While we were there a full moon
shone in all its glory on these glowing walls,
which the devoted love of an emperor raised
to his beloved one—"the Exalted of the
Palace "—Mamtaz-i-Mahal, and where he too
has built up his everlasting rest. To Mr. Smith,

the head-gardener, who is a Yorkshire man by birth, and has been chief of the Taj gardens some dozen years, is due their beauty and preservation; when first he came here these now splendid gardens were but a wilderness. More than once we saw the Taj by moonlight, and here are my impressions thereon:—

"Last night we enjoyed that fairy-like scene, the Taj by moonlight—a beautiful vision that beggars all description! It made one talk in a whisper for fear that the enchantment should fade and vanish like some wondrous dream. Ye gods, what beauty! The moon in her zenith, the line of fountains flashing like a million diamonds, relieved against the deep green of the cypress, the scarlet of the bougainvillea, and the purple leaves of the ponsetias; the interior of the temple all aglow, blue and red lights colouring the vaulted dome, around which a thousand spirits seemed to be whispering in endless harmony!" The fortress at Agra is stupendous without, huge walls within, a maze of palaces; it is more striking in size and situation than that of Delhi. This fortress was held by the British for four months during the Mutiny, while all the rest of the country was overrun by the rebels. Dr.

Roach, who knows every stone in the place, took us over this great work of Akbar, and explained everything about it; it is now under restoration, a work that appears to be conscientiously done. Besides the Fortress and the Taj at Agra, there are many monuments worthy of being thoroughly seen. Crossing the pontoon bridge over the Jumna, you come to another architectural marvel, the Mausoleum of Edmadood Dowla; its once beautiful gardens now allowed to go to decay, and its fountains are dry. It is a marble palace although full of tombs, the graves of Persian princes. Here the inlaid work is very beautiful, especially the inlaid floors, which are like superb carpets, but carpets of different-coloured marbles. The lower portion of the towers are octagonal, and in this detail superior to those of the Taj. Akbar's tomb at Sikandra, erected by his son Jehangeer, is a prodigious mausoleum, and has a park of splendid trees around it. At the summit of the building, and in a marble pillar, standing at the head of the emperor's grave, the Koh-i-noor was placed. A long day, in fact many might well be passed among the ruins of Fatehpoor Sikri, distant some twenty miles from Agra, which was the Windsor and Versailles of Akbar. The palace is surrounded by a wall five miles in circumference, and within are court after court, palace beyond palace; and a gigantic mosque, which Fergusson styles " Akbar's Grandest." The whole place is stupendously majestic. Within the centre of the great mosque is the marble tomb, with walls of solid marble, that reminded me in their detail and perfection of the Five Sisters' windows in York Minster. For hours we wandered through the glorious old place, so full of beauty that we felt a deep admiration for the people who have left here such match- less remains of a civilisation that might have made Athens and ancient Rome envious.

Leaving Agra on the evening of the 12th (January), we passed Cawnpore in the early morning ; but here we did not stay. There is not much beside the melancholy relics of the Mutiny to see there, and Marochetti's Angel, that folds her wings over the terrible well, I had seen ere it left England. We reached Lucknow on the following day.

" *Lucknow*, 13*th January*.—We are here in the cantonment, one of us in Airlie's, the other in ' Joe ' Lawley's respective bungalows, both belonging to the gallant 10th Hussars, whose mess is close by. We have been

C

sight-seeing all day. The places connected
with the year 1857 are the lions of Lucknow.
Of these, the principal is the Residency, held
through the summer of 1857 by Henry Lawrence against such terrific odds. The English
have done well to leave these ruins untouched ;
the place is eloquent of a struggle of which
every Englishman must always feel proud.
No nobler names adorn the military glory
of England than those so closely connected
with these battered walls : those of Lawrence
and Havelock. Lawrence died in the house
close by the gate of the Residency, called
Bailey's Guard. Other places of interest re-
lating to that terrible time is the Observatory,
where a massacre of English residents took
place ; the spot where Neill fell ; and the tomb
of Havelock in the Alumbagh garden. The
public buildings here are disappointing, and
have a theatrical and Brighton-Pavilion look
about them, and even the famous Chatar
Manzil and Kaisar Bagh palaces are tawdry,
although the latter cost £800,000. The
mess of the 10th was a most enjoyable and
hospitable one ; I was rejoiced to meet there
an old friend "Brab." Colonel Wood and
the other officers showed us every attention,
and overflowed with hospitality. The beau-

tiful Botanic Gardens of Wingfield Park
should be seen by all travellers to Lucknow;
the trees there are superb, and there are roses
in it which are wonderful. Leaving the
hospitable 10th on the evening of the 15th
(January), we reached Benares the next
morning.

"*Clark's Hotel, Benares,* 16*th January.*
—This is a clean and comfortable place,
with a show-room attached to it, full of graceful native iron-work, vases of a hundred
shapes and patterns. We have visited most
of the temples and sights, of which by far
the most striking, indeed one of the most
impressive of any that we have seen, is the
view of the city from the Ganges in the
early morning, when the natives descend
the endless flight of steps which lead down
from the piled-up buildings and temples into
the sacred waters in which they lave their
dark forms, is a memorable sight. Here
one can form some idea of the strong hold
that this people's religion has on them in
this their holy Kasi or metropolis of Hin-
dooism. It would require a very sanguine
missionary to hope that even in centuries
to come these 'benighted Hindoos' will
cease to believe in the sacred efficacy of

their ancient river, as it reflects the old
towers and spires of the temples of their
gods, and the blue smoke wreathing itself
to heaven from the funeral pyres on which
their dead are being consumed. It is a
sight one would wish to see again and
again, so weird and strange, and so totally
unlike any other scene that any country
but India could produce. We went out in
a row-boat pulled by natives, passing along
that wonderful succession of Ghauts crowded
by thousands of people, many bathing in
the sacred river. Old men, women, and
children in every conceivable coloured gar-
ment, were there. It out-Turnered Turner;
but what a picture would he not have made
of this! Above towered lofty palaces and
cone-shaped domed temples; the river,
too, seemed alive—craft filled with natives,
bearing large straw-plaited umbrellas in
junk-like boats—a scene that personified
the religious manners and habits of the East,
painted on a great living canvas. Returning from the river we came across some
of 'the lights of the harem'; at least we
were told that within some gorgeously
embroidered covered palanquins, escorted by
a mounted guard of wild-looking lancers,

clothed in green, and attended by some highly adorned footmen carrying silver sticks, were the ladies of the Rajah's harem; they had been bathing in the Ganges. Most of the temples at Benares are filthily dirty within; but the Monkey, and the one of the Sacred Cattle, as well as that in which stands the holy well, should be visited; also the Observatory, from the top of which one commands a general view of the city."

A twenty hours' railway journey from Benares lands the traveller in Calcutta. There we remained a week, guests of the Viceroy (Lord Ripon) at Government House, which combined all the freedom of an hotel with a splendid hospitality. We had arrived at an interesting period. The much-abused Ilbert Bill was passed while we were in Calcutta; and whatever its consequence may be, I have no doubt that the measure was one which Lord Ripon held to be one of justice and for the good of our Indian subjects. The time will come when the unpopularity among the Europeans in India which on more than one occasion broke out at Calcutta in disgraceful displays of personal antipathy to Lord Ripon will be forgotten, it is to be hoped. These people behaved like insolent schoolboys to

the Queen's representative, merely because
he had done what he considered his duty
toward the people of India. That it could
not have been a pleasant task to carry through
a policy under the circumstances of the
Viceroy all must allow; but in spite of the
gross insults and even threats of personal
violence, Lord Ripon acted the noble part of
a public servant of the state, placing above
popularity what he considered his duty, and
scorning to be bullied by the vulgar threats
and the personal malice of a set of men who
found that by giving more justice to the
natives they would lose some of their prestige
and power in the country, for which their only
feeling is how to get out of it as much as they
can in order to leave it the soonest possible.

Calcutta, when even a guest of the Viceroy, is not an inviting place. It contains no
architectural wonders like those we had lately
visited, and owes its fulsome epithet of the
" City of Palaces " to as hideous a collection of
stuccoed buildings and public offices as is
our wont to build. Government House, the
plan of which is, I believe, taken from Lord
Scarsdale's great house in Derbyshire, Kedle-
ston, has within some handsome rooms and a
fine hall with a double row of stately columns.

At the end of this gallery is a gaudy drawing-room, where the throne is placed. Here durbars are held. We saw one of these functions. A little princelet—little in size if not in wealth—the Maharajah Charati, was here received in state. His Highness appeared to be about twelve years old; a guard of honour was present, and a salute of eleven guns was fired in his honour, and the superb bodyguard, of magnificent native giants, draped in scarlet, were drawn up on either side of the Marble Hall, where they looked most picturesque. His Excellency was seated on the throne, and as the little prince approached, stept forward a few paces (these are counted ; so many for such a prince, and so many more for one of higher rank), after which both Viceroy and Maharajah seated themselves, and a short conversation ensued. The lad spoke tolerably fluent English, but seemed somewhat alarmed, which was not to be wondered at.

The Exhibition was in full swing while we remained at Calcutta, and this we visited often. Exhibitions have a monotonous sameness, and with the exception of the different native courts and the products of the different provinces, some of which were most beautiful, there was

not much of interest.  Here, too, I found a
great-nephew, Edward Clough Taylor's boy—
a sturdy little chap, aged two, with much of
the Campbell type in his little face, and with
bright curly yellow locks.

There was much of Oriental splendour
combined with English comfort at Government
House.  One evening a ball was given in
the Hall of Columns.  Some thousand guests
had been invited, but many kept away, owing,
it is said, to the Ilbert Bill affair.  I made
the acquaintance of Mr. Ilbert at the ball, and
was surprised to see a comparatively youthful
man, with a pleasant expression and intellec-
tual head.  I had expected at least an ancient,
grey-headed senior.  What was most marked
at this Government-House ball was the ab-
sence of good looks among the ladies, and
the very ancient ones who walked through the
quadrilles—these the wives of judges I was
told, and they looked it!

One morning with my relatives we went in
a steam-launch to Barrackpoor—the Viceroy's
villa on the Hoogli—some sixteen miles from
the city.  With the exception of the grounds,
full of fine trees, there is but little to see at
Barrackpoor; the Botanical Gardens, which
are considered the finest in India, however,

well deserve several visits; there the palm trees are superb. Leaving Calcutta in the early dawn of the 27th of January, we reached Madras three days after. Our vessel was a small P. & O. steamer, the *Teheran*. On board was the talented actress Geneviève Ward, on her way to Australia for a six months' engagement. The sea was as calm as a lake, but the heat rather overpowering. Although there was but little surf at Madras we had to be landed on the backs of natives; the new pier is half destroyed. Madras was preparing for the arrival of the Viceroy on his way to Hyderabad. We found little to take up the short time we passed on land at Madras, and on the following day took leave of India.

# CHAPTER III.

## CEYLON.

THE 1st of February found us half way between Madras and Colombo. On the next, the blue hills of Ceylon were close on the " port bow," and some of the passengers affirmed that they could sniff the " spicy breezes " that blew off " Ceylon's Isle," but I was not so fortunate. All day we have been running in sight of that lovely island.

> " To them who sail
> Beyond the Cape of Hope, and now are past
> Mozambique's, off at sea north-east winds blow
> Sabean odours from the spicy shore
> Of Araby the Blest."

By " Araby the Blest " did Milton refer to Ceylon? Probably, as before the Portuguese occupation it was under Arab rule. With the exception of Majorca, Ceylon has the loveliest line of hill and mountain that I have seen from sea—the nearer land green as an emerald, with distant hills fading into the ether. We entered the harbour of Colombo on the night of the 2d February, and landed next morning, rowed in by swarthy natives, a finer set of men than the Indians; but wearing their hair long, with combs stuck into their chignons, gives them a somewhat effeminate look.

Sir Arthur Gordon, the newly appointed Governor, made us at home at Queen's House, as the Government House here is called. His kindness and hospitality was unbounded; and under his roof we passed some of the pleasantest days that we had experienced since leaving England. Queen's House is large, with a garden at the back opening on the sea on the rocky beach. Sir Arthur, who is passionately fond of swimming, has had a swimming-bath cut out in the rocks, which proved a most delicious bathing place in this everlastingly hothouse-like climate. It was an additional pleasure on arriving here to find the late Governor, Sir William Gregory, here on a visit, an old acquaintance when together in the Commons. He reigned here some ten years ago, an universally popular Governor. It was pleasant to see the warm and hearty manner in which he was welcomed in Ceylon. It has been my good fortune to know the three most popular Governors of their time, all three Irishmen—Lord Dufferin, Sir Hercules Robinson, and Sir William Gregory. The latter was here when the Prince of Wales visited Ceylon. Ceylon being the first of the Crown colonies, Sir William ranked next to Lord Northbrook, "a very big swell indeed," as he expressed it ; "but when my time was up," he said, "I returned to England, to find myself only a simple Irish landlord who couldn't even get his rents paid him !"

Here, too, I met Major Knollys, who I had seen at Sydney, and who, when with Sir Arthur Gordon in Fiji, had greatly distinguished himself in the fighting there. On the following day Lord and Lady Rosebery appeared, on their return journey from Australia to England. They had but a day to see Colombo, and another to visit Kandy, and they certainly made a good use of the short time allowed them. With him I paid a most interesting visit to " Arabi the Egyptian," as he always styles himself. He lives in a little bungalow some three miles from Queen's House, pleasantly placed among well-wooded grounds, and cool from the sea

breeze. He is tall and of a dignified pre-
sence ; has well-shaped hands, and a remark-
ably good manner. We sat in a simply
furnished sitting-room opening out on the
entrance. Arabi can hardly say more than a
word or two in English, but we made our-
selves understood through a young Egyptian
who acts as his interpreter. He said that
there was no possibility of the Soudan being
conquered, even were the Egyptian Government to be backed up by England and
Turkey ; that the enthusiasm of the followers
of the Mahdi will carry everything before
them ; that the Egyptian troops, officered
by Englishmen, are considered to be outlaws
and outcasts by the faithful; and that the
probabilities are that in the end the Mahdi
will be able to establish himself as sovereign
over the Soudan. The slave trade, he affirmed
was and is supported by the powers that be
in Egypt, against the Mahdi's people.

On leaving him he said that he had not
passed so agreeable a time as he had done
with us since his arrival in Ceylon. This
is probably a form of Oriental civility ; but
civility, whether Oriental or not, is always
agreeable, and we were both, I think, agree-
ably surprised by Arabi, who is very far from

being the man that English correspondents during the Egyptian campaign made him out to be. He gave me the impression of having the welfare of his country at heart, and as far as one can judge by one interview, he has more the Kossuth element in him than that of a free-lance or filibuster. A few days after this visit he called at Queen's House, and spoke with evident gratification at having been called on by Rosebery; he was also full of gratitude to Sir William, whom he said is his best friend.

We had arrived at an auspicious time at Colombo, for an elephant kraal had been organised in honour of Sir William's visit, and to this the Governor invited my friend and myself. An elephant kraal is not an every-day or yet an every-year occurrence, as it requires great time to prepare, and many hundreds of men are employed in driving the elephant into the kraal, and these elephant drives are only given, as a rule, on the visit of some great personage, and all Ceylon is agog to see the sight.

We had been disappointed at not seeing the wild animals at Baroda; but we had now a far more curious spectacle before us, and I only regret that I am not more able to do justice to the great elephant kraal of 1884, which will long be remembered by those who were fortunate enough to see it.

*10th February.*—Since my last entry we have been out in the wilderness to an elephant kraal. We left Colombo early on the 5th. We—being the Governor, Sir William, Knollys, Murray (Sir Arthur's private secretary), and our two selves—we drove some thirty miles in a mail-cart, from the box-seat of which I had a good view of the splendid country we passed through. One can hardly exaggerate the beauty of Ceylon, and I doubt if there is any more beautiful country under God's sun than it; travellers who have been both here and in Java, however, give the latter the palm. We passed along a good road, bordered by every variety of tropical plant, through forests of cocoa-nut palms, and by valleys brilliantly green with rice and maize; blue hills rise in the distance, their sides covered with graceful foliage.

At the end of our thirty-mile drive, having reached a path leading through the jungle to the camp, we mounted horses, and rode half-a-dozen miles to our destination, a lovely valley named Yogama, where an encamp-

ment of bamboo-built huts formed a right-
angle. In front of that destined for the
Governor and Sir William seven elephants
were drawn up in a line, and salaamed and
trumpeted their respects in a most polite
manner. Close by the camp is a stream
flowing into a lovely pool; here the amphi-
bious Governor was soon swimming. This
pool is named Duhwaka, which, we are told,
meant in Cingalese, the pool in which you
must not fish. However, next day the pool
was fished, but with little result.

Up by six next morning, but the elephants
were still miles away, and watching the
natives drawing the pool of Duhwaka took
up the morning. The heat was intense, and
even only watching this fish kraal was hot
work; but a prettier sight than we saw that
morning I have rarely seen : hundreds of
natives grouped on the rocks and all around
the pool, in which the nets gradually approached one another, until the moment
came when, with great excitement, the men
pulled them ashore, and the fish were displayed dancing and struggling, their scales
glistening in the bright sunshine.

Early next morning we climbed the hill
before the camp, wherein lay the kraal, a

cleared space of two or three acres or so in the midst of the forest, strongly palisaded all round, so that not even a rush of the imprisoned elephants, an event which sometimes occurs, could break through this stockade. Two rough stages commanded a view over the kraal, looking like a very gigantic circus; the smaller of these stands was close to the only opening in the stockade, an opening some six feet in width, through which the elephants are driven. Our party were sheltered by a screen of leaves. Great care has to be taken that the elephants should not see anything beyond the stockade. The least sound or sight of anything that would excite their suspicions would make them turn and disappear into the jungle; therefore for several hours, and until the great fish were netted, we hardly exchanged a word, and never above a whisper. It was noon before the approaching cries of the beaters warned us that the elephants were at hand. The shouting, which at first sounded like distant cheering, now gathered volume, and seemed to come from every side; the excitement grew apace; soon the welkin rings with the shouts of seven hundred natives; there is a wild stampede around, a noise of branches

D

being torn and trees uprooted, and suddenly below us four elephants in a desperate state of excitement come tearing through the jungle, and make right for the opening in the stockade.

All four enter, and before long seven others follow their comrades into the kraal; the natives rapidly close up the entrances, and to all intents and purposes these great monarchs of the forest are made captive.

The following day we returned to the kraal, where the whole day was spent; and a most interesting one we passed watching the captured elephants being noosed. Four tame elephants were introduced into the kraal, and it was a most curious sight to see the intelligent way in which these four helped the natives to capture their wild companions. Owing, it was said, to some ill feeling between two sets of the noosers, a great deal of time was lost before the elephants were secured. The first caught was a female, and gave much play before the thick cords could be got round one of her hind legs. At length this was accomplished, and the second safely fastened; but by a great effort she snapped the ropes and broke away. When first captured her little calf had remained by its mother's side, indignantly shrieking at the proceedings; but on finding that its mother was a "captive," I regret to say the little one left her to her fate, and rejoined the others. At length the lady elephant was again caught, and this time finally; and later in the day another was secured. One of the most curious scenes was a fight between two of the tame elephants; they met in a narrow way, and refused to give way to one another; at length, after a great deal of roaring and pushing, one had to "throw up the sponge." Considering that the vanquished beast had no tusks and its opponent wore a formidable pair, this was not surprising.

There is no cruelty in this sport, only after the elephants are caught they are starved for a day or two until their ferocity has left them; after which, secured between two tame elephants, they are brought down to the plain, and become tame, it is said, in an incredibly short time. I was glad to hear that the English sportsman is no longer allowed to shoot these grand creatures, as he was too apt to do a few years ago. Not long ago one of these despicable, so-called sportsmen (and probably considering himself a gentleman), deliberately maimed and wounded half

a dozen or more of these elephants. Next
morning the kraal camp broke up, and we
returned to Colombo. During our ride,
which formed the first portion of our return
as it had been the last part of our expedition
to Yogama, an unfortunate accident occurred.
Murray happened to be riding by the side of
Knollys, who was mounted on a vicious brute,
which had a disagreeable way of letting fly out
its heels at the other horses; in an unlucky
moment Murray was struck below the knee,
and it was evident at once that he had been
badly hurt. He bore the pain most pluckily;
but was obliged to remain till a conveyance
could be got for him, and our otherwise most
enjoyable outing had a shadow thrown over
it. When we left Ceylon Murray was making
favourable progress, lodged in a delightful
little bungalow close by the Governor's House
at Kandy. My companion and I made a
pleasant end of the return journey to Colombo—in a boat, half raft, half barge, with
an awning, and gaily decorated with palm
leaves and king cocoa-nuts, that most
delicious of tropical fruits. In this boat, or
rather boats, for two canoes were joined
together, we were paddled by four natives
from a place called Kadu-wella some five

miles down stream to Colombo. A more
delightful mode of travelling than this cannot be imagined, floating rapidly down the
river in the gloaming, the banks on either
side clothed with foliage down to the water's
edge. About half-way down the stream we
landed to see a Buddhist temple at Kalenee,
one of the sights of Colombo. Thanks to the
initiation of Sir William Gregory, there is
now in Colombo a most admirably arranged
museum, in a handsome building, in front
of which most appropriately is placed a
bronze statue of its founder by Boehm. This
museum contains a very complete collection
of the fauna of the island, as well as a large
selection of native antiquities. Owing to the
short time we could give Ceylon, I was
unable to visit the ruins of the once great
native city Anarajapoora, of which Mr.
Smither, a distinguished architect, had just
completed a detailed survey. To judge by the
photographs of these ruins, they are of extraordinary interest and of vast extent. Mr.
Smither told me that he intended publishing
a work on this subject.

During the remaining week that we passed
at Colombo we had many opportunities of
seeing the strong feeling of attachment that

Sir William Gregory has obtained among the people of Colombo. One evening a great *fête* was given in his honour in a large compound in which an immense tent used for a ball-room had been erected, and in the ground around a variety of performances took place— fireworks galore, lamps more numerous than ever glowed at Vauxhall, and "devil dances," in which natives attired as demons gyrated with marvellous activity. Among the crowd "Arabi the Egyptian," followed by a suite of Egyptians, was a conspicuous figure; but still more remarkable was a group of three men clothed in splendid robes, and wearing on their heads the most gorgeous scarlet and golden crowns, for hats they were not, and caps they would not have deigned to be called. These three Magi—and they looked uncommonly like some of the representations of the Wise Men of the East—I learnt were some Indian merchants named Pulle. Later on I was fortunate to see them *chez eux*, as we were kindly invited to their house in order to see the ladies of the family. We found the whole family gathered, and were received with much cordiality; the ladies were in full dress. We were shown the way in which they dress for a wedding, for visiting,

and when at home. Gorgeous beyond description was the bride's attire; but she almost
disappeared, so bedizened was her form with
jewels of silver and jewels of gold. The
Pulles are Roman Catholics; the head of the
family since my return sent me a coloured
photographed group of the whole family, a
pleasing souvenir of our time in Colombo.

On another day we saw an interesting
ceremony connected with the ancient religion
of the country—a distribution of prizes at the
Widyodaya College, a Buddhist seminary
founded in 1873. The Governor was received
by a perfect galaxy of venerable shaven priests
in yellow robes. The chief priest produced
some ancient missals and relics, after which
speeches were delivered and prizes bestowed.

When it is remembered that Buddhism has
existed in Ceylon since the year 307 B.C. and
handed down in all its integrity since then,
one looked with more than a common interest
on these priests of the purest religion save
one that has existed—a religion that unlike
most others has not the stain of persecution
on its history. The Church of Rome might
have had a far less tarnished past to deplore
had it copied the far more humane tenets of
Buddhism. If one had not been born a

Christian, one would certainly have preferred the faith of Buddha to any other.

What made this prize-giving at the Widyodaya College additionally interesting is the fact that, although still unendowed, this college has already gathered under its roof pupils not only from Ceylon, but from other Buddhistic countries, from Siam, from Burma and Cambodia. Its two principal objects are that it should be a training school for Buddhist priests, and for the encouragement of the study of Oriental literature.

Floreat Widyodaya!

We had been fortunate in making the acquaintance of the chief of the police at Bombay, and again at Colombo found in W. George Campbell, who is the chief of the police in Ceylon, a most agreeable and pleasant person. A great affection for strange pets seems one of Campbell's strongest tastes. On visiting his pleasant villa we found a young crocodile in his bath, and one of the strangest and most uncanny little creatures in his house; this was a lemur, a creature half bat, half monkey, with the longest legs, that made it look like a gigantic spider; but the most remarkable thing about this animal was its face, which looked like that of a wizened dwarf with beautiful bright human-like eyes. One evening we were invited to a banquet given in honour of Sir William Gregory by Chief-Justice Dias. Some of the native gentlemen were attired in an odd naval-like uniform that had been introduced into the colony by the Dutch. I there made the acquaintance of the Chief-Justice's nephews, whom I found most intelligent youths; one of these is now study-ing at Cambridge.

Our stay in Ceylon ended with a visit to Kandy, a two-days' expedition. Those who have only seen Colombo can form no idea of the wonderful beauty of Ceylon unless Kandy is visited. We started at 7 A.M., reaching Kandy at noon. The far-famed railway line up through the hills merits its reputation. Nothing indeed can be imagined much love-lier than the views one gets from the train over the rich valleys as one ascends in zig-zag fashion the hills; tea and coffee plantations are far more beautiful than vines or olives. At the station of Kandy a dozen native chiefs were waiting to welcome Sir William; their costume was most remarkable, with head-dresses like idols, and with piles of brilliantly coloured satin wound round their haunches, a kind of glorified knickerbocker, doubtless a fashion brought into this country with Mynheers the Dutch. The Governor has a delightful place at Kandy, yclept the Pavilion —surrounded by hilly grounds and a paradise of a garden, where we found Sir Arthur, who had preceded us, with Lady Gordon and his A.D.C.'s. We were much delighted with a glorious red flower that I never saw anywhere before, named the amherstia. Sir William Gregory, who is very fond of Kandy, and to whose good taste and liberality when here as Governor the place owes much, took us over the walks at the back of the Pavilion, many of which he laid out himself. The views over the country from some of these are perfect dreams of beauty; and were it not for the heat, which is most trying, and the snakes, leeches, and other vermin, Ceylon would indeed deserve to be called an earthly paradise. The Buddhist temple is the great show place at Kandy, but after the Indian these Buddhist temples appear very insignificant. The Kandy botanical gardens are about as fine as those in Calcutta, and have what the latter have not got, great clumps of bamboos, some quite one hundred feet high.

During our stay at Ceylon we had a Singalese servant to look after our things.

Should any traveller be able to get G. D.
Sarnalis, I can strongly recommend him, a
first-rate valet, quiet, obliging, and attentive—
as it seems the Singalese in service always are
—and decidedly honest, which is a contrast
to the servants one is generally obliged to put
up with in India.

# CHAPTER IV.

## JAPAN.

WE left Ceylon on the 19th February in the P. & O. s.s. *Clyde*. There we met the Honourable T. R. Plunkett, with wife and family; two delightful little girls of twelve and six. Mr. Plunkett was on his way to occupy his new post of Ambassador at Tokio, in succession to Sir Harry Parkes. In every way Mr. Plunkett's is an admirable appointment; he is another instance of an Irishman being the right man in the right place. However, being born in a country does not make one a native of that country, and although we can call such men as Dufferin and Plunkett Irishmen, they are not really Irish merely because their ancestors settled in Ireland two centuries ago. The real Irish are the Roman Catholic peasants that have been in Erin since the times of the legendary

St. Patrick, a race as alien from our own as are the Laps or the Poles, with two hopelessly irradicable feelings firmly fixed in their character,—a hatred of the Saxon, and a love for the most idolatrous form of Christianity, the Church of Rome; that curse of many lands.

On the 22d we passed the island of Acheen, and next day at noon entered the harbour of Penang. Landed in sampans, native boats, and drove inland to see a water-fall, beautifully situated in the hills behind Penang. Penang is a picturesque town, with suburbs of villas each within a bright garden. Many of the houses are built on piles; but whether this is as a protection against the floods which are here frequent, or as a safe-guard against the reptiles, I do not know.

The view from the hills over the town and harbour is not unlike that of Naples. Vesuvius was represented by a large hill in Sumatra, and the whitewashed town carried out the resemblance. Leaving Penang the same evening we rather suffered from the heat, which seemed greater than any we had under-gone in the Red Sea, and many of the male pas-sengers passed the night on deck. Off Singa-pore on the morning of the 25th. Landed, and got rooms in Hotel de l'Europe; full of French, military and civilians, drawn hither by the neighbouring war in Tonquin. An uninteresting town is Singapore, with wide streets, having a semi-European, semi-Chinese appearance. Visited the gardens of a merchant named Wimpol; there the chief curiosity are some "Victoria Regia" lilies, growing in long ditches.

*1st March.*—We have at length entered into an infinitely cooler atmosphere, a relief after having been in a more or less liquid state of body these last three months. Our voyage since leaving Singapore on the 26th has been of the calmest, although some of the ladies have shown great determination in being more or less ill, reclining on chairs on deck, and being unable to descend for meals. We have a musical set on board—half-a-dozen men who are said to be "bell-ringers;" one of these is a good pianist, and nightly accompanies Captain Orme Webb, who sings well, and with what old Braham would have called much "entusymusy." The two little Plunkett girls, Nora and Nelly, are great favourites with crew and passengers; it would not be easy to find two nicer or better brought-up little sprites than they.

*2nd March.*—At noon we were at Hong-Kong harbour, where I found myself for the second time; so that now I have been " round the world," a very easy and pleasant job now-a-days. We have had a capital run from Singapore, two hours under five days, "the quickest passage in a P. & O. s.s," say the initiated. Our ship's gun was fired at noon, and much surprised the pious Hong-Kongers, then in church, for we were not expected till to-morrow at earliest. As I thought when here the first time, Hong-Kong is one of the most beautiful harbours and places. I see now no reason to change that opinion, although fresh from lovely Ceylon. We got rooms in the Club. Called at Government House on Sir George Bowen, whom I knew when Governor at Melbourne in '78. When last here Pope Hennessy reigned. I showed my companion " Happy Valley " and other beauties of the place. Sir George is cordiality itself; we dined with him and his family at Government House. Sir George as vivacious as ever. After passing four pleasant days at Hong-Kong, we left it on the 6th (March) in the *Kashgar.* Unluckily, a fog interfered with the view of the Ly-y-Moon Passage, a beautiful reach of sea and land. On the 8th we entered

Nagasaki harbour; the fine rocky headlands
of Japan seemed to welcome us, and I felt
greater delight in landing again in Japan than
I can describe.    There is not much to see in
Nagasaki; the principal curiosities are the
shops in Desima quarter, one of these a
china store (Koransha's), as large as Goode's
huge emporium in South Audley Street; in
a temple-yard a life-size bronze horse, effective and spirited, not unlike some of the
horses from Herculaneum in the Museum at
Naples.    Near this temple large camellia
trees were in full bloom, and the gay pink
almond blossom gladdened the eye on all
sides.    A violent storm of rain coming on,
we lay all night in the harbour and steamed
away next morning.    In the afternoon we
entered the narrow straits of Shimon-tseki,
the commencement of the inland sea.    The
moon, just past its full, shone down on a
beautiful scene of hills and waters, but it was
not till early next day, thanks to being roused
at cock-crow by Captain Webb, that one
could form an idea of the extraordinary beauty
of this matchless inland sea.    We were
threading its narrowest part.    Scores of
islands lay all around, the mist of the early
morning half concealing the villages nestling at

the foot of the hills ; the sea dotted with junks, looking like flights of large white butterflies. On the right rose a distant range of grandly shaped snow-covered mountains, the Shikolin range. As the sun rose higher the mist disappeared, and the fair scene had an air of enchantment. I should strongly advise travellers to get their first impressions of the "Land of the Rising Sun" by approaching it through this inland sea : they will then understand the intense fascination that Japan holds over all who have visited it—a land so unlike any other, so quaint, so beautiful, and yet so homelike in many respects. We reached Kobe in the afternoon of the 13th (March), and found most comfortable quarters in the Hiogo Hotel, kept by an Englishman ; not only clean, but luxurious. There is little besides this good hotel to detain one at Kobe, and on the day after our arrival we went on to Kioto. A week or more might well be passed at Kioto, but we were timed to remain there but a couple of days. Here, as everywhere in Japan, except at Yokohama and Tokio, passports are necessary ; these we got from our consul, Mr. Troop. A railway is open between Kobe and Kioto, a couple of hours' run between the two places. From the station at Kioto you have to traverse the entire city in jinrikishas, the little single-place carriages drawn by men, generally two to each carriage. We tore along the dimly-lighted streets at a great pace, by the side of what seemed an interminable canal, and at length up a hill, and finally were pulled up at the entrance to the Ya-Ami Hotel, more of a Japanese building than our hotel at Kobe. The view from the balconies of the hotel are very extensive, and all Kioto lies below like in a panorama; at night the hundreds of lantern-lighted streets look very effective.

*15th March.*—We have had a splendid day for a very pleasant expedition. Starting at nine this morning in jinrikishas, we went some fifteen miles to Oigowa — passing through the town with its densely peopled streets, out into the country, along rough and rutty roads, through hilly defiles, by the side of clear streams, and in and out of fir-wooded dales. Much of the scenery through which we passed reminded me of Scotland. At noon we reached our destination (Oigowa). There we embarked (carriages, men, drivers and all) on board a large flat-bottomed boat, and soon were shooting down the river, among rapids, narrowly passing in and out of rocks against any of which our bark must have come to signal grief. A most exhilarating mode of travelling we found this rapid shooting, and the skill with which the boatmen steer clear of the rocks is a sight to see. Accidents seldom occur; but that they do sometimes was proved by the broken remains of one of these flat-bottomed boats which had run on a rock. One of the passengers was drowned. An hour of this boating brought us to Arashyma, where we got luncheoned in a tea-house; thence by road some seven miles brought us again to Kioto. We visited some shops,—the silk and *curio* ones at Kioto are celebrated,—also a temple where is a huge bell, said to weigh some seventeen tons.

Our next expedition on the day following was marred by wet weather. The morning had promised well, and as one looked over the panorama of the town, the sun shining on the dark-wooded, fir-clad hills, one thought not of the possibility of rain; but the rain came just as we reached the shores of Lake Biwa, in the town of Otsu; and before we could get more than a general view of one of the most celebrated views in Japan from the Shintu Temple terrace, it came down in torrents,

and view and lake disappeared in a regular
Scotch mist, and there was nothing for it but
to return to Kioto. After visiting the large
Buddhist Temple, said to be the largest in
Japan, built entirely of wood, and containing
magnificent halls and rooms of state for the
Mikado, we returned to Kobe; and the
following afternoon were on board the large
paddle-steamer belonging to the Japanese
company—the *Midgi Bitchi* (Angl. Three
Diamonds), that runs between Shanghai and
Yokohama. The captains and officers of
this company are mostly Americans; ours of
the *Tokio Mari* is a most agreeable one,
Captain Strange. Before leaving Kobe I
may mention that we met with much civility
from one of the principal European residents
there, Mr. Hazlewood, of the Hong-Kong
and Shanghai Bank. Early on the morning
of the 20th we were in front of Yokohama,
welcomed by a gloriously bright sun, and by
my friend G. R. He had secured rooms
for us in the Club—a new one since I was
here last in '78, a most luxurious place,
with large billiard rooms and bowling alleys,
a capital *cuisine*, and a very genial and
agreeable set of members, American as well
as English. During the earlier part of this

my second visit to Japan (my first visit, in
1878, had been one of only a few hours, and
on this occasion I was determined to see
something of the country) the weather was
most unfavourable, and the rain would persist
in coming down in torrents. Here when it
rains the coolies who draw the jinrikishas
look like animated hayricks; their heads and
bodies down to their bare legs are all straw-
covered, but whether this is waterproof in
such tropical-like rains as we are having I
cannot say. I have already alluded to the
great attractiveness of the "curio" shops at
Yokohama. I found them as tempting now as
when last here, and Shobei's silks, and Musi-
sheer's beautiful artistic things in bronze, ivory,
lacquer, &c. are to me at any rate irresistible.
The days pass all too quickly in Japan. When
it is wet, these shops are the great attraction
here; when fine, endless expeditions can be
made. Alone properly to see all that is to
be seen at Tokio would in itself take several
weeks. I found at Yokohama old, and made
fresh friends; at Tokio, at the Embassy, were
the Plunketts, gradually installing themselves
in their new home; and at Yokohama the
Club was full of good company, and the
evenings went gaily by, bowls being the
principal attraction.

So bad was the weather that it was not until we had been at Yokohama a week that we got a glimpse of that peerless mountain, Fujiama.

*30th March.*—A red-letter Japanese day, for this morning I saw for the first time glorious Fuji. G. R. and I started off early for a long expedition on a splendid bright morning, a cloudless blue sky, and a breeze that would have exhilarated the poorest of spirits. Our "ride" was a succession of beautiful views and curious scenes, the grandest by far the great white mountain that seemed to come out bodily from heaven, and to be floating like an immense cloud, for which, had my companion not pointed it out to me, I should have taken it. On reaching Kamakura we left our jinrikishas and visited its solemn temple; the trees in the great yard in front, in full pink and white blossom, looking like showers of coral and pearl. We had passed by "the Plains of Heaven," a place deserving its name. Later we visited the great bronze idol of Dyboots, a hollow bronze representation, some sixty feet high, of Buddha in a state of Nirvana. We returned by the old Tokoito Road, along its avenue of fine old fir trees. Another day we were at Tokio, where we saw a wrestling match in

an open-air theatre, full of "local colour."
The Japanese of all sorts and conditions
much enjoy these sports. Except at a
French bathing-place, I have never seen
such grotesquely hideous fat men as the
wrestlers were; their fat lay over and about
them in huge folds; wrestling it could hardly
be called, as when one fat, semi-nude man
had pushed another off the platform, his was
the victory. Another pleasant visit at Tokio
was to Captain Hawes, head of the Japanese
School of Engineers; he took me over the
Mikado's Gardens, more like a park than a
garden, containing within huge walls many
acres of highly ornamented grounds, with a
race-course, a lake, and a cascade, and with
many pretty gazebos and tea-houses scattered
about. The still unfinished Japanese Club
we visited also, a large and very handsome
building, furnished in European style, and
with a good ball-room. After dinner at
Captain Hawes's,[1] an old Japanese lady
painted in an inconceivably short time a
number of fruit, flower, and bird subjects with
infinite skill and effect.

My next outing with my friend G. R. was
among the hills, some fifty miles from

[1] Joint author with Mr. Satow, H.M. Consul at Bur-
mah, of the Guide to Japan, published by Murray.

Yokohama. We tiffined at a tea-house in the village of Fujisawa, and reached Tonasawa at the foot of the hills towards dark. In a prettily situated spot close by the river was lodged an Italian artist, Sig. San Giovanni; he has passed months there, and has made some capital pictures of Japanese manners and scenery. After leaving Tonasawa I tried a new form of conveyance, being carried up the hills in a kind of box called a "kango," supported by poles on the shoulders of the coolies. As the darkness increased, one of those men walked ahead with a flambeau composed of sticks. At length our destination, Kiga, was reached, a little village among the hills on the edge of a rapid stream. This was my first experience of a night passed in a Japanese hostel; the walls of paper, and paper screens for partitions. How Carlyle would have abhorred such a dwelling, where every sound is heard, as if the occupants of the house lived in one common room! We were up betimes next day, and walked over the hills to Hakone, a glorious walk in fine weather; but we got it wet, and when we reached the sulphur baths of Ashinaga it poured in buckets. A curious sight are these baths. In a long building are a row of baths, full of Japanese, male and female mingled

indiscriminately: it reminded me of the
public hot baths at Buda-Pesth. After
Ashinaga we had a long tramp across some
bare hills, like parts of Inverness-shire. We got
into Hakone thoroughly soaked, and put up
at a large tea-house on the shore of the lake.
When travelling in Japan it is necessary not
only to take food but one's bedding with you.
I found that sleeping on the floor of these
tea-houses was not uncomfortable, although at
first the want of any chairs or tables is somewhat a nuisance; but after all, these little in-
commodities make up a good deal of the
novelty of seeing life in Japan.

The next day, too, was wet, but over the
hills we had to go to reach Atami, some sixteen miles off. We crossed over an endless
hog's back of a mountain, from which in clear
weather there is said to be a fine view of the
sea; but we saw nothing owing to the heavy
mist and rain. I should advise travellers not
to visit the Japanese highlands until May.
The descent on Atami is even on a wet day
a pretty sight. On the right, bold headlands
jut out into the sea, and lying in front is the
volcanic isle of Hasshima. At Atami we
found some friends, and shared their quarters
in a little tea-house. Atami is a great place
for invalids to come and bathe, and the

natural hot baths are in great vogue here.
Many of the richer Japanese have recently
built villas at Atami, where they come and
pass the bathing season.

Returning to Yokohama on the following
day, we skirted for upwards of four hours
the sea, along a road that reminded one
of the Corniche, and certainly as beautiful.
We were again in jinrikishas, and at a high
speed we passed by a lovely panorama—the
hills on one side, the sea dotted with islands
on the other, and in and out of villages, gay
with the blossoming gardens, and bright with
the blossom of the plum and cherry trees.

At the village of Odawaru we left the
" man-power " carriages, and drove into Yokohama in a trap along the Tokoido road.

Off again next day on another expedition
to Nikko. " Those who have not seen
Nikko," say the Japanese, " have not seen
Japan," and certainly, if time permits, a visit
to Nikko is one that all travellers should
make. My friend and I went first to Tokio,
where we embarked in a little tub of a steamer,
and where we passed the night in a cabin
only four feet high; so that even sitting
upright was a difficulty. However, like other
things in travelling, it was an experience, and
we managed to pass the night tolerably com-

fortably. Slowly we ascended the shallow river, full of boats manned by men in blue dresses, the banks thickly covered with bamboo and with many a village. At four o'clock next morning we reached the little village of Koga. There we disembarked, and after breakfasting started off in jinrikishas to Nikko, a journey of fifty-five miles. It took us thirteen and a half hours to do it. The state of the roads from recent rains was deplorable, and at places it seemed a matter of impossibility that the coolies could get us over them; but these wonderfully wiry fellows did their work in splendid style, each pair of jinrikisha coolies being relieved by others at almost every half-dozen miles on the road. We arrived at Nikko after dark; men came out with lanterns as we neared the place. The finest portion of the road is when Nikko is approached. An immense avenue of gigantic cryptomerias, said to be a century and a half old, look most imposing. Some of these trees must be at least eighty feet in height. Nikko itself is beautifully placed among pine woods, and surrounded by fine hills—like a bit of Switzerland, or of the Engadine. (Suzuki's Hotel at Nikko can be recommended.)

Temple visiting was the order of the next day, and this place being the Walhalla of

Japan, its temples are not only remarkable for great beauty and elaborate decoration, but for national interest, and the extreme beauty of their situation. The finest temples are those of Sambutsudi, with its great gilt figures of the three Buddhas; the superbly ornate group of temples called Iqe-Yasu, which exceed even those at Sheba in lavishness of decoration, with it wondrous well and pagoda, and above the mausoleum amongst huge stone pines. The finest sight I thought was the view looking back through the archways from the courtyard of the Yashamon Temple. We met near here a crowd bearing grotesquely carved and gilded shrines up the temple stairways, looking like a scene of a very magnificent open-air pantomime.

Leaving Nikko early next day, we had a glorious walk of eight hours over the hills to Ashiwo; splendid scenery all the time. Over and over again I felt as if we had suddenly come into Switzerland; even the cottages with their timbered roofs covered with stones strengthened this impression.

We passed that night at the village of Ashiwo, in a little inn named Ityunyu. All next day we walked through a superb country skirting the river Wataraseyawa, a bright rushing stream of a deep bottle-green colour. Near the village of Sauri the scenery is magnificent. Huge boulders of rock lay hundreds of feet below us, around and over which whirled and eddied and rushed the torrent. The hills about here are very grand; patches of bright pink blossom, wild-cherry trees probably, relieving the somewhat sombre tone of the fir trees. At Sauri we luncheoned on some delicious little trout fresh from the river, excellently well fried by Matsu our guide. We got into the picturesque little village of Goto, still in the highlands, by dusk, and found comfortable quarters in the little inn of Tamaya, with its artistically painted ceilings and (paper) walls. An odious little maid disturbed our slumbers at five the following morning by tearing open the screens that here serve as walls and shutters between the different rooms. After this sleep was impossible, and there was nothing for it but to pack up our mattresses. We sped on that day many a mile in jinrikishas, for now the hill country was passed and we were back again in the plain. Crossing about noon a wide stream in a ferry-boat, we soon after reached Kumagaye, from which place the rail is open to Tokio. And so ended our pleasant expedition to Nikko, which I strongly recommend to all those who like a good walk over the hills, and can put up with the trifling discomforts at the different tea-houses on the road.

My stay in Japan was now drawing to a close, and I have but little more to add to these scattered notes of one of the pleasantest journeys I have ever made. Before leaving Yokohama I was invited to a garden party given by the Mikado at Tokio. Japanese royalty has imitated ours even in this respect of giving a large party and at a very trifling expense. Much as I dislike all functions, I felt it would be a mistake not to go to this one, and accordingly having invested in a tall hat, which is as obligatory on these occasions as are tights at our Queen's court, I went to the capital, calling first on the Plunketts at the Embassy. From thence we drove through the city to a large enclosed garden close by the railway station. Passing through a pavilion-kind of building, one entered the royal demesne, the most notice-able feature there being an artificial lake studded with islands connected by the main-land by wooden bridges. What made the gardens really beautiful were the quantity of blossoming trees—"summer snow," as the Japanese happily call it. The deep-purple brown of the maples contrasted well with the white and pink blossoms. I cannot say that the invited guests added any beauty to the scene. Most of the Japanese, and all the men, wore European costume, and looked like mutes at a funeral. Some of the Europeans wore "pot" hats, and the general look of the company was decidedly dowdy. There was an interminably long time to wait before His Majesty deigned to appear, and when he did we beheld a short and very insignificant man, in a German kind of uniform, followed by half-a-dozen Japanese ladies—princesses? These were good enough to give some local colour to the scene, being dressed in their very becoming national costume. The Mikado moved on slowly, like an automaton that had been somewhat feebly wound up. The ladies of the court had their faces thick with paint; the people gathered round them, and the Mikado had some difficulty in moving along; the crowd cringing and cutowing to him, seemed as much the fashion here as in our own country, and I noticed the same forced leer on the eager faces of those nearest to the sovereign, looking as hungry for a nod as a cur for a bone.

The last night I passed at Yokohama the American Consul, General Van Buren, gave a farewell dinner. The General himself is one of the greatest human landmarks of

Yokohama, a fine specimen of the best type of American, with a patriarchal head and a snowy beard, but as bright in spirit and keen in humour as a lad of twenty. The press was represented by Mr. Brooke of the *Herald*, the *Times* of Yokohama, but without the tediousness of our ponderous print; nor must I omit the *Punch* of Japan, conducted and illustrated by Wyman. It would take too long were I even to give a list of those who I may still hope to meet again in the " Land of the Rising Sun." On the morning of the 27th of April I watched from the bows of the P. & O. s.s. *Oceanic* the "peerless mountain" fading away over the waters, and fervently hoped that it was not the last time my eyes would rest on Fujiama. I have now but to wish all that may have read these notes, in the gentle, melodious Japanese language, a hearty

SAYANARA.

(

www.ingramcontent.com/pod-product-compliance
Lightning Source LLC
Chambersburg PA
CBHW020304090426
42735CB00009B/1221